WHAT WOULD JOHN DO?

BIS Publishers
Het Sieraad
Postjesweg 1
1057 DT Amsterdam
The Netherlands
T (+) 31 (0)20 515 02 30
F (+) 31 (0)20 515 02 39
bis@bispublishers.nl
www.bispublishers.nl

ISBN 978-90-6369-235-3
First published 2010

Copyright © 2010 John Altman / BIS Publishers

Written by Will Georgi
Told to Will by Hajo de Boer
Illustrations by Jeroen Klaver / Shamrock (www.shamrocking.com)
Cover design by Gummo

All rights reserved
Printed in China

BISPUBLISHERS

FOR MY PARENTS

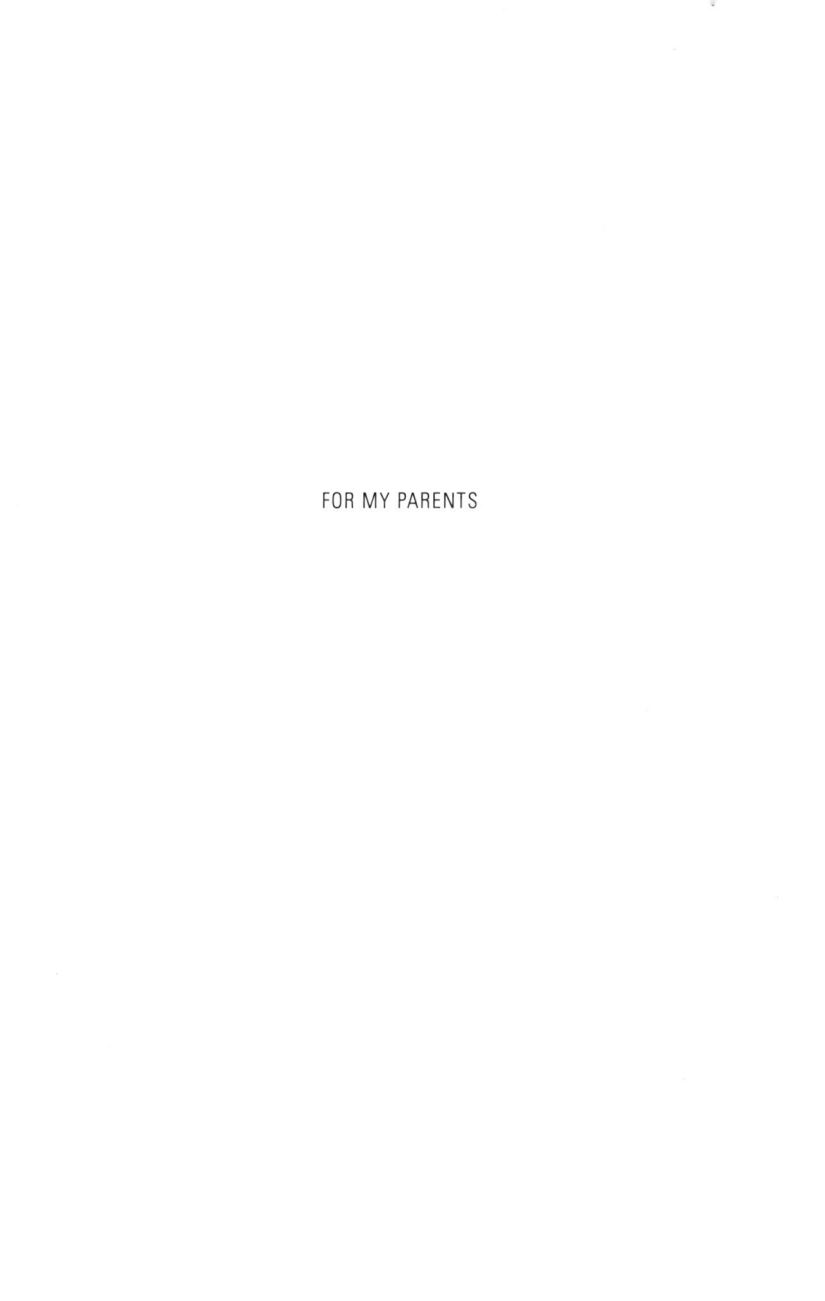

CONTENTS

INTRODUCTION THE NAME'S ALTMAN, JOHN ALTMAN 6

INGREDIENTS WHATEVER, MAN 14

PREPARATION YOU'LL NEVER BAKE ALONE 30

THE KITCHEN HOME IS WHERE THE HEART IS 42

MAKING DO LESS, GET MORE DONE 54

BAKING IF YOU LOVE SOMETHING, SET IT FREE 66

AFTERWARDS THERE ARE TWO SIDES TO EVERY COOKIE . . . 80

EATING BON APPÉTIT! 94

EPILOGUE SO WHAT NOW? 104

A NOTE ON THE AUTHOR(S):

In the now infamous winter of their discontent (otherwise known as 2007) two Dutchmen disillusioned with their lot in life (it turns out there are only so many times you can go to the Van Gogh Museum or have your bike stolen) embarked on a journey around the world in a quest to find their true destiny.

Instead they found John Altman, who revealed to them the mysteries of how a humble cookie contains all the ingredients for a happier life.

Upon their return to the Netherlands, they started to bake cookies and to spread the word of John far and wide. News of the phenomenon reached even as far as England and the ears of a young romantic who travelled across the perilous straits of the North Sea to hear the tale straight from the horses' mouth.

This is their story…

The

name's Altman, John Altman.

INTRODUCTION

The name's Altman, John Altman. Unless you're one of the lucky few to have had the pleasure of his company, you could be forgiven for wondering just who on earth John Altman is. We wondered exactly the same thing when we first met him on Baker Beach, San Francisco. Back then, he was just a man with a beard and an infectious grin strolling along the beach with a tray of cookies, wearing nothing but an apron and a pair of dog-eared flip-flops. We were entranced. Especially after he offered us a cookie.

It might have been the sun, it might have been the gentle sea breeze, it might have been the intense combination of melted butterscotch and freshly squeezed grapefruit, but John's were the best cookies we'd ever tasted. So damn good, we had to ask him if we could take them home with us. "Sure dude," he said, "spread the love."

John invited us to spend a few days with him at his place. He baked, we ate and then – not long before we parted - he gave us the recipe for his cookies, along with his blessing to make them around the world. His gift showed precisely the measure of the man – to pass on his life's work to us and ask for nothing in return except to make other people's lives better. John had asked us to "spread the love." So spread the love we did.

Since those carefree days in San Francisco, we've tried to follow John's exhortation in every part of our lives. We bake cookies, use natural ingredients, try to make everything we do have as little impact on the environment as possible, and give 10% of our profits to good causes. In short, we follow the seven steps laid out in this book. A book that will strive to portray the man – no, the friend – we got to know: a man completely at ease with himself and the world, who never let anything worry him and radiated harmony to everyone lucky enough to cross his path. We'll try and capture the magic of those all-too-brief days we spent together with John and leave you with an impression of the man vivid and striking enough to inspire you to ask the same question we ask ourselves whenever faced with a dilemma: What would John do?

At the risk of immediately disappointing you, we're afraid that

without the great man here to answer for himself, there can never be a definitive answer to "What would John do?" But answers are overrated, anyway. There are dozens, if not hundreds, of books out there that profess to give well-meant advice on how to live your life more successfully or provide "answers" to the big questions in life, whatever they may be. This book isn't one of them.

One thing that we can guarantee John wouldn't do is spend all day or night reading self-help books or take himself far too seriously, if at all. In John's book, life is for living and enjoying, not spent searching for answers whose questions are irrelevant in the first place.

If there's an answer in this book, it lies in those three words John left us, "spread the love." They serve as our guiding light in his absence, a light so bright that it illuminates even the darkest of days. What would John do if someone cuts in while he's waiting patiently in line at the bar? What would John do if his bike gets a flat tyre and he's running late? What would John do if he gets fired or dumped? (Unlikely, given that he's never had a job, but not all of us can be that fortunate.) We don't know. But when we think of John, we know where to start looking for answers. And if, even then, we can't find those answers, we just go and bake some cookies.

See, the wonderful thing about John's mantra is that it's a broad gospel. It covers every step in the baking process, but that doesn't mean its message should be confined to the kitchen alone. As John was fond of saying, what we do in the kitchen echoes through eternity.

John passionately believes that cookies are the ultimate way to spread the love. They're easy to make, and even easier to share. They can help you meet new people, tell old friends that you love them and bring people together. They're especially good for cheering you up on a day when nothing else seems to be going your way. That's the power of the cookie. And you'll discover just how potent a force for good it is as

Since those carefree San Francisco days, we've tried to follow John's exhortation in every part of our lives.

we help you make the perfect cookie. How? By doing what John would do of course….

We'll guide you through every step of the baking cycle, with the same mix of sage advice and questionable humour that John favoured us with. You'll discover how to assemble and grow the right ingredients, how to put yourself and your kitchen in the right state of mind, what you need in your kitchen and what you don't, how to make, bake and shake your cookies, and what to do afterwards.

And by the end of it all, we'll have something truly special on our hands and in our stomachs. So sit down, make yourself comfortable, and we'll begin…

WHAT WOULD JOHN DO?

INGREDIENTS: WHATEVER, MAN

What would John do? Well, he'd probably start at the beginning. With cookies, and what goes into making them. As you'll have gleaned from the cover, John's is a recipe book with only one recipe. That means you get to decide what you want to make and we're fairly relaxed as to what ingredients you choose (finally, a cookbook that caters to every taste). Contrary to what some doubting Thomases might believe, this isn't because we're too lazy to come up with lots of recipes ourselves, but because John showed us that a recipe comes from inside you, not from the pages of a book. We can help you on the way to finding your destiny, but ultimately you have to walk your own path yourself.

It's common knowledge that you are what you eat (and we can certainly confirm that after we spent a week in Turkey only eating kebabs), but John took it to the next level by suggesting that what you bake is what you are. What you put in the cookie reflects your personality and your feelings at that particular moment in time. So anything goes. Feeling blue? Blueberries. Or perhaps a double-triple chocolate chip cookie for the ladies. But being in the privileged position of having access to all ingredients in the world can be a bit overwhelming at times.

Apparently the human brain can't handle more than seven choices at any one time, meaning that the luxury of choice, whether in the greengrocer or the internet superhighway, can lead you on a road to nowhere rather than to enlightenment. So we'd like to share a few pointers that John passed on to us to help you get to grips with the eternal mystery of what John would put in his cookies.

TO EACH HIS OWN

There are a lot of different ways to seek inspiration for the key elements of your cookie. For example, if you're feeling a touch lazy, you might want to go with an established favourite. This is the classical, or old school, approach to cookies. There's a cute Dutch proverb to support this course of (in)action, which goes a little something like "it's better to steal something good than come up with something crap yourself." I mean, chocolate chip cookies are everyone's favourite for a reason. They simply taste very, very good indeed. Millions of people can't be wrong. Unless they're at a U2 concert, but

INGREDIENTS: WHATEVER, MAN

Our city-based society is in danger of losing sight of what food actually is. Even someone enlightened as myself can be tarred with this brush, as I used to think tea actually grew in teabags.

then not even the grand sum of John's accumulated wisdom could save them from eternal damnation. So don't feel guilty about following tradition and choosing to bake a classic cookie. If that's how you feel, cool.

However, we would strongly encourage you to search yourself and your cupboards for the contents of your cookies instead of instantly and brazenly resorting to theft, or "borrowing" as John preferred to term it. Like the time he "borrowed" fifty dollars, a quart of beer and a bike from us before he rode off into the sunset. Despite our deep wellspring of affection for John, that really took the cake. However, you'll be pleased to hear that's one lesson we'll allow you to skip.

Coming back to the cookie, sometimes you just need to let the past (and the fifty dollars) go and move onto something new. It might be hard, it might involve a bit of thought, but to quote another Dutch proverb, if you never shoot, you'll never score. Take your chef's hat off for a moment and replace it with your thinking cap, at as jaunty an angle as possible. After much research, we found the most effective way to bring out your creative side is to remove yourself from every other form of activity and concentrate solely on the task at hand. Some people call it meditation. We call it "special time." To fully clear one's mind, John would suggest the following course of action:

1) Quit your job.
2) Go back to bed.
3) Wait for inspiration to strike. (N.B. This may take some time.)

Or, if this all sounds a little extreme, you can always do what John did the first time we went back to his house. As soon as we were happily ensconced in his kitchen, John asked if there were anything he could get us. "Beer (please)," said our resident alcoholic. "Hmm, a Hershey's bar?" said the slightly more gluttonous of our duo. "Sure," John said, "whatever, man." But instead of giving us what we'd asked for, we watched flabbergasted as he poured them into a mixing bowl and proceeded to make beer and caramel bar cookies. Fortunately, it all ended happily every after. The cookies were delicious, even if they did smell a little strange – a bit like walking into a bar the morning after you've had one drink too many. No matter how much you love beer, that can be a bit hard to stomach. Especially at ten o'clock in the morning.

So before you worry too much about what flavour cookies to make, sometimes it's worth considering the direct route and reaching for whatever's in your larder and whacking that in. That pack of dried apricots may have been on the shelf for a while, but it doesn't make them any less worthy a match for those almonds you've just roasted. While buying and trying new things is always exciting, you should never underestimate what's under your nose. Why use imported mangoes flown over (and frozen) from the other side of the world when the cherries in your garden are ripe for the picking? Why sup concentrated and pasteurised orange juice when you can make the real thing yourself in a few seconds? It's simpler. And it's better.

GO NATURAL

John never buys things in cartons or boxes. Well, maybe canned beer once in a while. Or wine in a box at the weekend. But that's about it. He follows a strict see-food diet – never eat anything your great-grandmother wouldn't recognize as food. Natural is as natural does. John wholeheartedly embraces going natural as a philosophy and way of life. So much so, that when we first met him all he was wearing was a pair of flip-flops and an apron. It would appear that giving away cookies is harder work than it looks. Though fret not; nudity is strictly optional when it comes to making cookies. All that being said, we would strongly advise you to wear an apron during the later parts of the baking process.

Health and safety concerns aside, going natural is important on a wider scale. At the moment, our city-based society is in danger of losing sight of what food actually is. Even someone as enlightened as your correspondent can be guilty of this particular sin: I used to think tea actually grew in teabags (which if you think about it actually makes some sort of twisted sense).

Today it's possible to buy oranges already peeled, coconuts already shredded. And the meat supermarkets offer is about as far removed from the animal it allegedly originates from as it's possible to get. Some chicken breasts I've seen have more water in them than the beer served at student unions. Even cookies aren't exempt. If you're brave enough to go through the litany of items in the cookies you buy in the store, you'll find at least fifteen ingredients, most of which would be appear to be more at home in a chemistry lab than in your mouth. But if you make cookies

Growing your own ingredients will keep your larder stocked with fresh ingredients all year round and your mind overflowing with fresh

at home, there are only five basic ingredients. Butter. Flour. Sugar. Eggs. And whatever mouth-watering combination of ingredients you've chosen as the icing on your proverbial cake. Now that Great-grandmother Gertrude could approve.

Unlike the time a popular TV chef quizzed a classroom of kids to find out what kind of vegetables they recognized. Nine times out of ten, the answer was "carrot." They simply didn't know any others. So even after the carrot had been correctly identified, leeks, courgettes, cauliflowers and broccoli were all branded as carrots too. Funny as it may have been, that's simply not healthy. We need to take pride in our vegetables, and everything else we grow, to preserve nature in all its glory and variety. It's one thing not to know that peppers come from a plant because the weather's too bad for them to grow in London, but another thing entirely not to even know what a pepper is. Good things grow on trees. Ideas, fruit, vegetables (yes, for all the pedants out there, a plantain can be classified as a vegetable), everything.

Starting your own garden, no matter how big or small, is the first step to getting back in touch with your roots in nature. And if you want to have a "dress down Friday", John-style, to get in the mood, we're right behind you. At least in spirit.

GROW YOUR OWN
The fresher the ingredients, the better your cookies will taste. We're not suggesting that you make your own butter, sugar or flour (everyone has their limits) but if you can grow your own staple ingredients your cookies will taste all the better for it.

John's a big believer in growing your own – it's cheap, there are no shady dealers (or supermarkets, as they've come to be known) to go through and it's an infinitely more rewarding experience. Growing your own ingredients will keep your larder stocked with fresh food all year round and your mind overflowing with fresh inspiration: Lemons in September, Strawberries in June, Pumpkins in March (if you've got a greenhouse) and Rosemary in January, to name but a few. To decide what you want to put into your cookies, all you have to do is stick your nose in the garden, and voila!

You'll also have the added satisfaction of nurturing your seeds from packet to plants to cookie. You can check on their progress every day, give them a little water, even have a quick word with them every now and then. If it works for Prince Charles, it will work for you. And the best thing is that if you

> You can check on their progress every day, give them a little water, even have a quick word with them every now and then.

look after them properly, they'll give you back their very best – and for years to come. Yep, we love plants. As we'll discover, there's much you can learn from getting back to nature. But what's of vital importance in this instance is that a good baker should know exactly what goes into his or her cookies. And that's where your garden comes in extremely handy.

The best part is that you don't even need to have a garden to grow stuff. In fact, if you're a devotee of Vertical Gardening, you don't even need any earth to grow some plants. But, if you're operating on a slightly more down-to-earth budget we'd suggest you invest in a couple of window boxes, or even just reuse some plastic containers or old saucepans, put some earth and seeds in, and watch them grow. You might not consider your humble piece of earth significant, but oh, boy, it is. If you live in a city, not only will you be transforming a bleak urban space (no offence) into an infinitely more pleasant natural environment, you're encouraging plants to bloom and wildlife to flourish. All with a simple herb garden or tomato plant or tree. Biodiversity never tasted so good.

BALANCE THE SWEET AND SOUR

If there's one rule that we will insist on in this book (well, insist is a big word) it's this: When contemplating what should go into your cookies, you have to balance the sweet and the sour. It's not because we're fascists, or even fussy, simply that in our experience you can have too much of a good thing.

Too much sweet = bad; too much sour = bad.

It's about finding the right balance. It's interesting how words like "sweet" and "nice" – compliments when applied to food – sound distinctly ironic when applied to people. There's no bigger sinking feeling than when you're trying to woo somebody and the object of your affections brushes you off with "aah, how sweet." Equally, there's no fainter praise than "Oh, yeah, she's, er, nice."

It's rather strange, since we all want to be nice people and do things that other people would consider sweet, yet when confronted with someone who displays exactly these traits they become unattractive.

It's like Cliff Richard. Your mum probably loves him, and your granny too. And probably her granny as well. He's had a number one record in every decade since time began, was a rock 'n roll pioneer, does some work for charity, is a good Christian boy and by all accounts is a very nice man. But I can't stand the guy. He's just too, well, nice. If it were a tossup between spending an hour with him and someone as utterly repugnant as Silvio Berlusconi, I'd genuinely struggle as to whom to choose. At least Berlusconi might have you put you out of your misery earlier.

While we're not suggesting that Cliff and Silvio are the ideal dinner party guests (unless you're a particularly vicious masochist or wholehearted humanitarian), their presence should nudge you towards heeding the necessity of considering what each ingredient brings to the party and how their differences need to be accommodated. So the next time you're tempted to add an extra spoonful of sugar to make the medicine go down, just remember Cliff and throw some chillies in as well.

JOHN'S FINAL THOUGHT
If being a hippie means anything, it's doing whatever you feel like, and doing it proudly. One man's lemon is another man's orange.... You know what I mean.

If not, the important thing is that if you like something, you should do it, regardless of what other people might say. The same people (including us) that turned their noses up at John's legendary Black Pepper & Rose flavour when first offered it, now profess it's the best cookie they've ever tasted. We're not sure what it was that first got up their noses about that particular taste sensation, but it just goes to show that you should always follow your own nose and not let others stick their noses in your business. Even if you think you've dragged out an idea about as far as possible, Lord knows someone, somewhere, will find it funny. And if it makes just one person smile, it's all been worthwhile (I love you Mum).

So trust in yourself, your instincts and your ingredients, ignore the haters and it'll all come good. And whatever you do, don't forget to put in the most important ingredient of all. Love, man. And lots of it.

PREPARATION: YOU'LL NEVER BAKE ALONE

John may not have been a boy scout (he never could deal with authority) but he was always prepared. Always. To stress the importance of being ready for whatever life might throw at you he would quote the old Chinese proverb, "Before setting out on a journey, dig two graves." At least we think that's what he said. What he actually meant is anyone's guess. Anyway, his point (we think) was this: Whatever you do, you have to be ready before you begin doing it. It might surprise you that such a famously laid-back man would take something as superficially trivial as cookies so seriously, but that is to underestimate both the man and the cookie. For if something's worth doing, it's worth doing well. Especially if it's making something that you're actually going to put inside your mouth (insert your own crude gags here).

A wise man (not John for a change) once told us that everyone has one talent that they're the best person in the world at. Someone somewhere plays Bach on the piano like nobody else (except maybe Johann Sebastian himself). One lucky devil will write the best self-help book ever written, while one young buck drives the fastest milk crate in the West.

At first it appeared that John's gift was the ability to put anything (no matter how urgent) off until tomorrow. Closer inspection revealed that John's lax approach to timekeeping was, in fact, due to his intricate method of intense and methodical preparation – and as we learned, preparation is key when it comes to baking.

TAKE YOUR SWEET TIME

By now you should have worked out what you're going to put into the cookie, but before you do anything else you need to make sure that the main ingredient in the cookie-making process is in the right place: You. So sit yourself down, stick the kettle on and take a minute (or five) to make sure you know exactly what you're doing. For what you're about to embark on is a life-changing experience.

Yes, you heard us. The cookies you're about to bake will change your life.

PREPARATION: YOU'LL NEVER BAKE ALONE

No one thinks it's unusual for an athlete to prepare for four years to run ten seconds at the Olympics, so why should it be strange to wait a little while to bake some cookies?

Cookies can make the world a better place. This isn't half as grandiose as it sounds, because when you consider the bigger picture, everything you do changes your life a little bit, and somebody else's too. Changing the world means doing lots of little things that (when combined) can have a big benefit. What starts out with a cookie baked in San Francisco could go as far as the White House. Why do you think everyone always goes round there for tea and cookies? John was fond of saying that the thaw in the Cold War began with a cup of Earl Grey and a particularly fruity oatmeal cookie. Now that's something to chew over. We hope you'll never underestimate the humble cookie ever again.

So no matter how much you might want to bake the cookies right now, it's vital to take the time to fully prepare yourself and gather every single ingredient, pot, pan, baking tray and lucky rabbit foot you'll need to bake the best cookies ever. Otherwise who knows what might go wrong. Whether it's going to the loo without having had the foresight to check your stock of toilet paper, or braving the great outdoors in England without an umbrella, galoshes and a distress flare, assumption (and lack of preparation) is invariably the mother of all, er, things that don't go quite right.

Therefore it should come as no surprise to learn that baking cookies was a process that John would wait days, even weeks before beginning. That's the sort of respect that the cookie engenders. No one thinks it's unusual for an athlete to prepare for four years to run ten seconds at the Olympics or to leave whisky maturing for twenty odd years to reach full complexity of flavour, so why should it be strange to wait a little while to bake some cookies? Especially if they're going to be damn good cookies. When it's time to begin, you'll know. And everything will happen more quickly because of it.

However, some poor misguided fools have confused thorough preparation with laxity. But there's a world of difference between waiting for the iron to be hot and simply having an appetite for production as meagre as Axl Rose. If you tend towards the latter camp, we would suggest that you start as soon as possible if you want to have the cookies (or anything in fact) clear this side of 2050. Unless of course you're reading this in 2051, in which case you'll think that's not at all long to wait and will probably have even less idea than the people of 2010 about who Axl Rose is. Lucky you.

FOCUS ON WHAT YOU'RE DOING

Thus thoroughly prepared, the one thing John would always enter the kitchen with was focus, absolute focus (and a glass of sherry on Sundays). Half-cooked he may have occasionally been, but nothing he ever did was half-baked. Quite apart from the perils posed by salmonella, that never works out well. You might enjoy the thrill of living on the edge, but trust us: it's not worth it. Chopping hazelnuts while checking how much ginger you need, watching a football match on TV and simultaneously having a conversation with your spouse might sound like a lot of fun, but adding this sort of spice to the baking process can only be perilous. There's no place for multitasking here.

Sure, combining pleasurable activities can make them even more enjoyable: John likes nothing better than reading and soaking in the bath; sitting on a surfboard and shooting the breeze; drinking and eating – or drinking and anything, to be fair, but this is neither the time nor the place. Multitasking might impress in the office, but it certainly won't impress the apple of your eye when you have to offer them soggy cookies after you spent too long on the phone during the vital whisking process. Handling one thing at a time is the patented Altman way to success. As John's neighbour would say, free your mind… and your ass will follow.

As we said before, cooking's a serious business, so you should focus one hundred per cent on the task at hand, whether it's for yourself or the benefit of others (unless you're a big fan of burnt or undercooked food – thanks to my Dad's culinary skills I still can't enjoy a sausage unless it's black on both sides). That doesn't mean that you should think only about cooking and nothing else while you're in the kitchen. It's a good idea to try and immerse yourself in the perfect atmosphere for baking. In which, of course, preparation is everything. The right music is a good start (John's partial to a bit of the Grateful Dead or TM Juke) but mobile phones are bad (unless you're using them to call your mum). Friends in your kitchen are good, Friends on TV is bad. Get the picture? You'll find an extensive guide to what you should have in your kitchen in the next chapter, but for now, empty your head (and kitchen) of everything that doesn't contribute to a conducive atmosphere for baking.

GET STUCK IN, BUT DON'T GET STUCK

Nothing in life is perfect. Not even John. John wouldn't want you to try to be perfect either. All he wants to do is help make your life and, indeed, everyone else's life, taste a little better. So while you should always prepare everything as best as you can, you shouldn't wait for the stars to align and for everything to be perfect, because sadly it never will be. Put simply,

PREPARATION: YOU'LL NEVER BAKE ALONE

over-egging the situation means you won't begin anything. So if you can't find any fresh basil, don't let it get in your way. Just use the dried stuff from a jar. And if you can't find Belgian Chocolate, Swiss is probably O.K. as well. Yes, it will be a different cookie. It might turn out better than what you'd originally intended, it might turn out worse. Whatever it is, it will certainly be more exciting. If it's good, you'll reap the rewards and plaudits, and if not, you can learn from what goes wrong. Ultimately, it'll still be a good cookie made by your fair hands that everyone will appreciate. And if anyone has the gall to complain that you used Swiss chocolate, they don't deserve to be your friend in the first place.

ANTICIPATION IS SWEET

Another of John's favourite proverbs (which by 2051 will have come to be known as "Johnisms") was "It's better to travel hopefully than to arrive." That's not to say that you should expect disappoint-

So when doubts started to creep in about what to do next, he rang up his dear old ma, who proceeded to help him prepare to make the perfect roast for his friends.

ing cookies – it's just that sometimes the anticipation can be just as enjoyable as the result, if not more so. The best thing about anticipation is that everything is still possible before you actually begin something, so at this stage you might as well sit back and dream. Tell yourself that these will be the best cookies you've ever made. Ever? Ever, ever.

The longer you indulge in this phase, the more pleasure you'll be giving yourself – and that can never be a bad thing. However we do have one word of caution for y'all: Christmas. See, building up the anticipation is all well and good, but keep in mind that what you're doing in the here and now is just as valuable as the event you're looking forward to in the future. Especially if it's a Georgi family Christmas. Sorry Mum.

ASK FOR HELP IF YOU NEED IT

Every morning (well, on both days we stayed at his place) John made us repeat the same two things:

No one is bigger than the cookie.

Don't bite off more than you can chew.

These words really brought home the fact (as if having five people in the kitchen hadn't) that cooking is a communal activity. If you're not too big to read this book, or look to John for advice and inspiration, you shouldn't be too big to ask your friends or family either. Asking for help isn't a sign of weakness, it's a realisation that other people can help you make something even better than you can. The big man asks, the small man doesn't, as John once succinctly put it. Asking for help is something that everyone gains from – people will be flattered that you've asked for their assistance, while you get to learn from their wisdom and experience. And it's always more fun to do something together than on your own.

John told us a story about the first time he cooked a nut-roast dinner for his friends. He had a rough idea of what to do as he'd seen his mom do it a hundred times, so when doubts started to creep in about what to do next, he rang up his dear old ma, who proceeded to help him prepare to make the perfect roast for his friends. She still brings it up twenty years later (thankfully no one at the meal brought up anything afterwards). It just goes to show the pleasure that you can give someone by enlisting their help. Because everyone loves cooking, especially when the end result is something delicious that can be shared together.

To wrap things up, just as you're not bigger than the cookie, neither is the cookie bigger than you. So don't worry if everything's not exactly as you want – if it's good, it's good enough. And if it's good enough for two, that's what we want to see. Go with the flow. Focus on the enjoyment and what you're going to do, because it's a beautiful thing and will make people happy. It may be ever so slightly cliché to say that it's the thought that counts, but that's only because it's true.

WHAT WOULD JOHN DO?

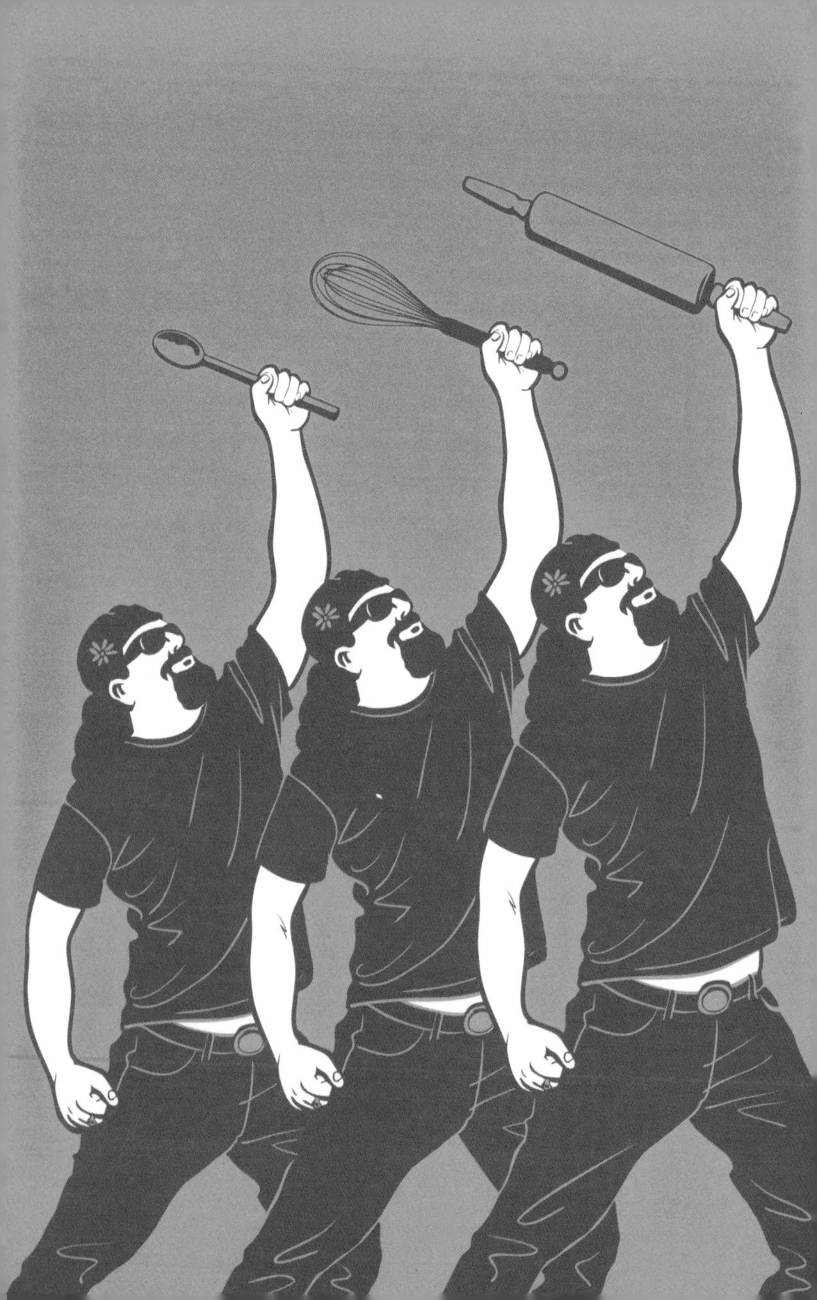

The Kitchen

Home is where the hearth is.

THE KITCHEN:
HOME IS WHERE THE HEARTH IS

Location, location, location. The kitchen may not be where you're from, but it's certainly where it's at. And in John's world, it's sure as hell the only place to be. I mean, if a rug can tie a room together, then a kitchen can tie a house together with both hands pinned behind its proverbial back. Anyone who's seen *9½ Weeks* knows how much fun it's possible to have in there, even without doing any baking. And it's surely no coincidence that every (good) party always starts and ends in the kitchen.

You could say that it's for the simple reason that the kitchen contains everything you need: food, drink and the facilities to make more of both if you so desire. It also has the distinct advantage of being the warmest room in the house – literally and metaphorically.

But it's neither of these benefits that makes the kitchen the most important place in your home. John always insisted that the kitchen was more of a womb than a room. More often than not he'd say this after one too many glasses of his homemade wine, as his 'r's loosened simultaneously with his trousers, slightly diluting the force of his eloquence.

But the connection between these two environments runs deeper than a labiodental approximant. Both are special places where we're proud to say the 'magic' happens, where everything begins with popping one in the oven before something tiny and incredible is brought into the world. The clear advantage cookies have is that you don't have to wait nine months for the end product, it's a lot easier to clean up afterwards, and if you aren't happy with what you've made, you can do it all over again.

John was like a pig in shit (his words, not ours) in the kitchen and proclaimed the kitchen table to be the centre of his universe (quickly followed by a disclaimer saying that it was really his current girlfriend/wife/favourite record/ spatula). But it's true. The kitchen offers a space and comfort

If there's one statistic that shows the moral and physical decline of a civilisation, it's how many people eat dinner in front of a screen.

unparalleled anywhere else in the known universe and is the ideal space to create something special in your home – but unbelievably, our kitchens are increasingly under threat.

SAVE OUR KITCHENS

In all of our travels across the world it wasn't Macchu Pichu, Reunion Island, Red Square or Alcatraz that most captured our imagination. Nope, it was the flat we rented in Manhattan, New York that didn't have a kitchen. These "homes" only have space for a microwave. The horror. Yet strangely, most people always manage to find space for a TV.

If there's one statistic that shows the moral and physical decline of a civilisation, it's how many people eat dinner in front of a screen (or two if you're a follower of the current vogue for watching TV whilst playing with your laptop). In some countries this figure can be as high as 72%. Ok, every now and then it's good to get a pizza in and stick the football or *Mad Men* on. But if you have friends and family around and you don't share time at a table while eating a homemade meal, you're depriving yourself of one of the most pleasurable and important things life has to offer.

Why do so many of us deny ourselves this basic human right? It's time to lose the TV and reclaim the ancient art of eating and the room that provides sustenance for our bodies and souls. It's our contention that a house isn't a home without a kitchen, so sharpen your knives and make ready to defend their honour. We unite under one banner to proclaim that the John Altman campaign to save our kitchens starts here! (After much practice we found that this rabble-rousing rhetoric works much better if you imagine us standing atop our kitchen table, striding to and fro, holding a fork or kitchen utensil of your choice, and jabbing it victoriously skywards. That's better, no?)

Membership is especially open to those people unfortunate enough not to enjoy the use of their own kitchen. Even when John was on the road lugging bags for a particularly hairy and popular 70's prog rock band (who, for legal reasons, we're unable to identify in this book) he still managed to keep on baking. Yep, some times, you gots to mellow slow. Takes time. Pick a place to go, then just keep on baking on.

When you're on the road (it's amazing how many stories John told that started with this particular gem) you learn to live with only what you can carry, beg, steal and borrow. Or ask for on the rider. John found that you could make food with just a stove, a bag and a lot of goodwill. Even now these are the main pillars of his kitchen. Obviously it's optimal (we have to sound professional every now and then) to have your own kitchen, and the bigger the better, but if that's not possible, then recreate one from what's available. Pop round to use a neighbour's stove, call your boyfriend to get the flour you're missing, ask your friendly local drug dealer for his knife. And if they ask what they'll get in return, the answer's simple. Cookies. And no one can say fairer than that.

MI COCINA ES SU COCINA

An open kitchen doesn't mean an extractor fan; it should mean that it's open to all your friends and family. After all, what's the first thing you do when someone comes round to your home? Offer them a drink or a bite to eat. And where does that come from? It's not that you need to have a fridge or garden comfortably full of things to offer your friends, but if you open your kitchen and your heart, then you'll reap the rewards. Your friends might even do the washing up for you afterwards.

So attractive has the kitchen become that word has reached us of a phenomenon in England where people pay to eat in other people's kitchens while the owners cook for them. While we applaud the idea, it's so much easier to do it for yourself. What they do for money, we do for free. For if you're opening your house to people, you should do it out of the goodness of your heart. Although making a bit of money on the side is just about defendable, especially if you invest the money wisely (charity, cough, cough).

John didn't have a lock on his front door and would leave it open during the day. But nothing ever got stolen, because people loved John and what he stood for. We're not suggesting you do the same (especially if you live in New York) but maybe we should all follow John's example and open our homes to more people more often. The one time there was a "break in," all his guests (John refused to call them criminals) did was throw everything on the floor. Which turned out to be a blessing in disguise, as John found the signed copy of *What's Going On* that he thought he'd lost forever.

So lock your door, and you'll end up locking your heart.

WHAT YOU SHOULD (NOT) HAVE IN YOUR KITCHEN

John's house could be described as the most stylish mess we've ever had the privilege of witnessing. It may have been full of bric-a-brac, and lord-knows-what from top to bottom, but it was good stuff: Books, records, candles, paintings, clothes, plants, and an especially impressive large wooden globe with a hidden liquor cabinet inside it. His bathtub came from a demolished Hollywood hotel, friends had given him his leather Chesterfield sofa when they moved and the dinner table was made by John himself from wooden pallets he'd found on the beach. It was a point of honour for John that there wasn't a single piece of furniture that he'd actually paid for. When he told us that, our minds wandered back to our own friends' (or our own) meticulously designed homes, with their vintage china, the specially imported Kenyan spotted bluestone tiles in their gardens, their alphabetically ordered bookcases and the design magazines that had brainwashed us into thinking that a home should look like an inhabited showroom. We'd seen *Fight Club*, and like Tiger Woods, we'd learned nothing. John's house might not make it into *Monocle* or *Wallpaper*, but it was full of love, and full of John.

John's kitchen, on the other hand, was a veritable study in functionality: nothing out of place and nothing that wasn't absolutely essential. While John would passionately contend that a Margheritaville shaker is indeed an essential item for every kitchen, he wouldn't feel the same way about the Megatron Supa-Dupa 3000 magic wand, or a celebrity endorsed "flavour shaker." Not even a knife from a village in Japan that's been blessed by the local village elder and washed in the blood of a thousand whales would find its way into John's drawer. Mainly because he's a staunch supporter of the WWF, but that's beside the point. These trinkets may all be the best on the market but come on dude, using them to make cookies is like driving a 4x4 in the Netherlands (which for our non-European readers is pretty much the smallest and flattest country in the world, uncannily similar in shape, if not form, to one of their most beloved gifts to the world, the pancake).

It's surely no coincidence that every (good) party always starts and ends in the kitchen.

Flights of fancy like this are stupidly expensive, and for another, they don't last. If you need any proof of just how transient they are, check out your local junk store and see how many of them are piled up in the back. They might make you a fortune on eBay in 2051, but this constant need to improve on what already works is simply unnecessary. Toys may be good for impressing your friends or fighting against the midlife crisis, but they won't help you make better cookies. No sir (or ma'am). Especially when they run out of batteries or the power gets cut off. And who's in control? Us or the machines? Get back to the old school and don't take a risk, use a whisk. Kaboom tish.

More to the point, baking cookies isn't rocket science. Therefore your kitchen shouldn't resemble a laboratory. It should look like a kitchen. People have been baking cookies without the Megatron Supa-Dupa 3000 for hundreds of years, so why start messing with that now? Stick with what you know. Your mum has a favourite rolling pin because it's done the job for her for donkey's years. As she'll no doubt tell you, trust is built on something firm and solid – not something quick and instant. So listen to your mum. She always knows best. That's because she's your mum and she's been excelling in that role for years. Toys and gadgets might be so hot right now, but they'll be forgotten in five years. So leave them on the shelf and get the hell out of the store. And whatever you do, don't look back. Besides their evident and manifold evils, these devilish devices also get in the way of cooking – you'll never learn if something else does the work for you. It might make things easier in the short term, but you should never trust the machines, man. They might claim to do things better, but ultimately you should trust yourself, not them, to do your best. It should just be you, your food and the hands. That's the only Magimix we're interested in.

Always remember:

THE GOLDEN RULE
Make your kitchen your home. Which means making it a place you love. The better you treat your kitchen, the more you'll get out of it. Fill it with things you like – no, love – and you'll want to spend more time there. Start with a stereo. Something nice to go on the walls. Maybe some books (like the one you're holding in your hands right now). Add a sprinkling of some friends and keep it clean.

And above all, don't fill it with crap you don't need.

4 MAKING

Do less,

get more done.

MAKING:
DO LESS, GET MORE DONE

You might find it a bit of a contradiction for a chapter about making cookies to tell you to do nothing, but that's exactly what we're going to do. Contradict ourselves. It's not the first time, and it certainly won't be the last. Sometimes that's just the way the cookie crumbles.

It's not like making things is bad; making love, for example, is wonderful. As scores of ladies have been told, it's natural to make a little something something. We've done it since we were kids; sandcastles, imaginary friends, a mess. And it was great fun. Now we're all grown up, the only thing we tend to make is mountains out of molehills. Which is exactly why we need to rediscover our capacity for making, for utilising our natural and God-given imagination and invention to bring amazing creations into the world. Like cookies. But how, you might ask. By doing nothing, we'd tell you.

Because if there's one thing that John would do above all others, it's nothing. For as he told us before we stepped into his kitchen: "The less you do, the more you get done." That still sounds as good to us as it did way back in sunny San Francisco. It sounds even sweeter when you take it to its logical conclusion, which is that by doing nothing, you can accomplish everything you could possibly desire. Success is that simple in John's book.

Unfortunately, we feel obliged to point out that doing less doesn't always mean doing nothing. Sometimes a man simply has to do what a man has to do. But the good news is that it means doing less of the stupid, unnecessary, unhealthy things that suck up your time and energy without you even realizing it. Like worrying. For one reason or another we spend too much time worrying about things that really don't matter. Did I put too much butter in the cookies? Have they been in the oven too long? Did I actually lock the door behind me? And was the window open? Is my zipper undone? If you spend too much (or even any) time worrying about these things you probably wouldn't even leave the house for fear of being run over or picking up a cold on the bus, or both.

And we should know. When we were staying in John's house, we were so scared by the responsibility of looking after his legacy, that every time we left his house we'd go back to check to see if we'd actually locked the door or not. This was, of course, particularly stupid given that John doesn't have any locks on his doors. One other time we were convinced we'd left the oven on, and cycled back for half an hour to discover that, yes, we had indeed turned it off. We ended up missing the first half hour of *The Hot 8 Brass Band* for that particular trifle.

Hard as it may seem, if you can cut worrying out, not only will you protect yourself from male pattern baldness or the early appearance of grey hairs, you'll have more time and energy for the more pleasurable stages of the baking process. Or life, as it's otherwise known. So you can just get on and make the cookies. Too much time spent worrying (or doing anything, in fact) is simply a waste of time. You might think you're spending your time staying late to earn extra cash, but there's only one kind of dough that can bring you real happiness. And it's not the paper kind.

IT'S NATURAL

If you think about it, this course of action makes perfect sense, as "nothing" is exactly what everything in nature does to reach its goal. And what comes naturally is easy and fulfill-

> *The possibilities for the advancement of the human race are endless: for a start, we'd have instant world peace, because apart from anything else, war's a lot of effort.*

ing. That's why it's called "natural." A tree doesn't try to be a tree, it just is a tree. A puppy doesn't try to grow into a dog, it just wakes up one day and feels like chewing the postman rather than the adorable stuffed toy you gave her a year ago. It's not rocket science. It's Mother Nature doing her thing. And she does her thing very well without any help from mankind, thank you very much indeed.

On a wider scale, the possibilities for the advancement of the human race are endless: for a start, we'd have instant world peace, because apart from anything else, war's a lot of effort. If you make love, cookies, or just chill the fuck out, the situation you'll find yourself in is peace. Which is lovely for all concerned.

But you don't have to take our word alone for the fact that removing yourself from life's rich pageant is the best thing you can do to ensure its success. Happily there's a much, much wiser man than us who's actually proved that letting nature get on with, well, growing and stuff, without people getting in the way is much more productive. Masanobu Fukuoka's (may he rest in peace) greatest gift to the world was "do nothing" farming. It's as wonderful as it sounds. Plant a few seed balls, leave them well alone, then come back and reap the harvest a few months later. And the best thing is that it works – to be fair, you do get less plants, but the ones that grow have a higher yield; the earth becomes more fertile; and you don't have to do a single thing apart from enjoy the fruits of your labour. For developing this wonderful system, Fukuoka has been hailed by far more reputable sources than your humble correspondent as a seminal figure "who distils philosophical and spiritual truths into a practical approach to farming." (Thank you Wikipedia). A bit like John and baking then, just without the practical part.

And if you need further convincing, allow us to get all Biblical on you for a moment. As it turns out, even

Fukuoka's greatest gift to the world was "do nothing" farming. Plant a few seed balls, leave them well alone, then come back and reap the harvest a few months later.

our homeboy from Galilee was down with doing sweet Fanny Adams:

"Consider the lilies of the field, how they grow; they neither toil nor spin, yet I tell you, even Solomon in all his glory was not arrayed like one of these."

(Matt. 6:28-29)

Fairly conclusive, I'm sure you'll agree. Do nothing, and you'll live like a king – and that from the King of Kings. Although I'm fairly sure that John would have preferred the metaphor of a bottle of wine improving with age simply by lying around in the dark and doing nothing for a long time, before coming out for a night (or afternoon) of good company and good food. That's the way it works in John's holy trinity of peace, love and baking. It's a philosophy that has led him to become one of the happiest people we've ever met, with more friends than we've baked cookies and a life dedicated to spreading the love. And he's achieved all this by doing precisely nothing. It's a course of (in)action that everyone, no matter their rank or status, should learn from. Now that's change we can really believe in. "But how on earth does this all relate to baking?", we hear you ask.

DOING LESS AND BAKING COOKIES

Well, once you've stopped worrying and learned to love the bomb, that'll put you in a better, and therefore more productive, mood to enable you to make a better cookie. Leave your frustrations at the kitchen door. Don't worry, be happy. Do what comes naturally to you (i.e. nothing) and you'll be in the right frame of mind to make your cookies.

If not, it's probably time to try the world's most productive form of doing nothing ever, Part Two. Yes, it's time for more meditation. Although it'd be slightly unfair to say it's doing nothing just because you spend a lot of time sat down motionless. That's what one of John's buddies who was particularly fond of John's cookies – the excessive consumption of which, in combination with his philosophic meanderings, gave rise to his name of Yogi Bear – taught us. His *Active Meditation Ashram* attracted devotees from all over the world. A day with Yogi Bear (at a competitively priced $450, including an all-you-can-eat cookie buffet) would begin with "sitting meditation" in the morning, followed by "walking meditation" in the afternoon, arriving just in time for tea at John's for "eating meditation." Of course Yogi Bear was with his pupils every step of the way, except for the walking meditation part of the programme which he preferred to supervise from his veranda while simultaneously deepening his knowledge of sitting and eating meditation, occasionally with a bit of "drinking meditation" thrown in if he was feeling especially in touch with his spiritual

side. Now that's what we call enlightenment.
So, meditating or not, obviously you should always give the cookie the time, love and attention your precious effort merits, but that doesn't mean that you have to make it more complicated than whacking all the ingredients together and dolloping the batter on the baking tray. It's as straightforward as it sounds. After all, a simple pleasure shouldn't be complicated. And the more you do it, the easier it becomes. Making a cookie, or doing anything you enjoy, isn't hard work. If it's related to any form of activity, it's a labour of love. And when you love doing something, giving it your all is as easy as pie.

Oh yeah…

As this is a cookbook, and this is the making chapter, you were probably expecting some actual tips on how to make cookies. We'll give you the best piece of advice we know. Ask your mum. See? Do less, get more done. Now, we're off for a drink.

Yogi Bear was with his pupils every step of the way, except for the walking meditation part of the programme, which he preferred to supervise from his veranda.

If you love

5 BAKING

something, set it free.

BAKING:
IF YOU LOVE SOMETHING,
SET IT FREE

HAVE A LITTLE PATIENCE

Normally, we don't have a lot of time for Sting – any in fact. Or any of the half-arsed musicians who have churned out the same nugget that we've pinched for this chapter's title a thousand times or more. But it pains me to concede that they may have a point when it comes to baking cookies. For now we enter the truly challenging part of our journey. Even harder than listening to *Fields of Gold* on repeat. Letting go. And we're not going to lie. It's going to be tough. You're going to have to be patient. Time may fly when you're having fun, but man, does it drag while you're waiting for the fruits of your labour to blossom from cookie dough into the cookies destined to bring sunshine into your life and joy to your taste buds.

LETTING GO

If you've been paying attention (come on, it was only a few pages back), you should be familiar with John's mantra of doing nothing to bring you whatever you want. But to really possess the object of your stomach's desire, you need to take it one step further by letting the cookies go. Completely. Absolutely. 100%. Wash your proverbial hands of the whole affair. And it probably wouldn't do any harm to wash your actual hands too, because they're probably a little bit mucky by now. For to acquire something, to really get what you want, you have to let it go and put it in the hands of fate – otherwise known as the oven.

What makes it especially difficult is that up until now you've been in charge of everything: what goes in the cookie, where you make it, how you make it, who you make it with. You'd be forgiven for thinking that all there's left to do is put your cookies in the oven. Easy, you might think. Wrong would you be, as everyone's favourite diminutive Jedi would delight in telling you. To be so close to having something, and then to let it go is one of the hardest things to do in life, but if you do can manage it, the rewards are bountiful. And what's more, you'll more be a man, my son. Or a lady, if you're one of our female readers. John doesn't do discrimination, even if Rudyard Kipling does. The only link John and Mr. Kipling share is making exceedingly good cakes (note to reader: Rudyard Kipling was a poet; Mr Kipling is a baker beloved in England for his *Fondant Fancies*. There's nothing quite as embarrassing as having to explain your own jokes, but we wanted you to appreciate every layer of this quite superb piece of prose. This isn't motivated solely out of sheer vanity, but to show exactly how hard is to let go of something, or "kill your darlings" as creative types like to call it).

THE OVEN IS YOUR FRIEND

As anyone lucky enough to have been to a teambuilding seminar will tell you, letting go is all about trust. Don't worry though, you'll find no lame exercises about falling backwards here – our insurance wouldn't cover it. In the kitchen you need to trust the oven, give it some space and allow it to produce the goods in peace, without you getting in the way. As John once told us: "If you bake it, they will come." It's the way of the world. Grass grows. The sun rises and sets, the moon waxes and wanes, the tides ebb and flow. Cookie dough turns into cookies.

We mentioned doing things naturally in the last chapter, but now it's time to pass through the gauntlet laid down by Chapter 5: to let things go, you need to let things happen at their own pace. And as hard as you might try, you can't make cookies cook quicker without turning the heat up and spoiling them. That's a problem not even John can help you with.

Because try as you might, you can't control everything. Man might try to be all-powerful and force the planet to obey him, but ultimately nature always wins. You can't even rule it by royal decree, as number two on the official WTF Top Ten Rulers of England Hit Parade (William the Conqueror was always the runaway leader), King Canute, tried and failed to show.

According to legend, and every good history teacher, Canute went down to the seaside (the start of the short-lived boom in English tourism) to show just how powerful he was by turning back the tides. Sadly for Canute, his resultant failure led to him being recorded in posterity as a bit of a (C)nut, when his real intention was to show that no one is more powerful than God. But that's what happens if you try and mess with the planet. We can mess with Mother Nature a little bit, but if you push her too far, then things will start going wrong, as we're beginning to discover.

By placing your trust in the oven, you're accepting your place in the world. There's simply nothing more you can do; all that's left is to disengage yourself. We told you about not worrying; now you'll learn that letting go of worrying about the past and the future, about what you've done and what might or might not happen, will help you to enjoy the present more. Yes, perhaps you could have made the cookies differently, and yes, they might not turn out perfectly, but there's nothing you can do about it now. Sometimes the oven will be too hot, once in a while the eggs will be bad or you might have taken Chapter One a little too much to heart and thrown in one handful of chillies too many. All you can do is chalk it up to experience and move on.

If you're feeling particularly daring, you can practice it now and just throw a plate on the floor. See, it's not that bad, is it? Or if you can't bring yourself to break your own crockery, invite your clumsy friend round (we've all got one, normally called Roger for some reason) and let him or her loose in your kitchen.

Anyway. Don't worry about what you can't control. We're all going to die at some point, and things will go wrong between now and then. This isn't *The X Factor*, this is real life. It's how you roll with the punches that matters. Although death's quite a tough one to come back from, we'll give you that.

WHAT YOU NEED TO LET GO

Over one particularly fruity cigarette, John declared that the cause of all suffering was craving and attachment. Actually, John didn't say that, Buddha did. And that's one man you'll never win an argument with. Whatever. What John really said was this: "Wanting stuff is just a waste of time. At the end of the day, they're just possessions. Here today, gone tomorrow." True, Buddha's thing might have been a little bit more poetic, but the sentiment was the same. The solution to suffering? You've got it: letting go. Accepting what is and what isn't and just rolling with it. Lesser men or women might see this as weakness. Not so. There's no higher power or mental strength needed than to rise above proceedings or earthly events. It's

> *You'd run down to the mailbox every morning to see if it had come, but if not, you'd wait safe in the knowledge that it would arrive in its own sweet time.*

like taking one step closer to heaven. This isn't being complacent, this is being practical. To take responsibility, you first have to let go.

Now that your cookies have been safely deposited in the oven, you've got about 15 minutes (depending on whether you like them rare, medium or well done) to do something else. It might not seem like much time to fill, but after you've invested so much in the making of the cookies, it'll seem like an eternity. You might find it frustrating. You might find it boring. We'd encourage you to find it fulfilling.

Think about all you've done, all you've achieved in your journey so far and all the joy there is to come, and as soon as you close the oven door, you'll be overcome with an intense feeling of contentment that will infuse your entire body and soul. If all's gone well, you should experience a lightness of being that will transport you back to your carefree days as a child, when you knew that everything, everywhere, in the universe would be alright. This sensation will be further enhanced once the cookies start to smell absolutely heavenly after a few short minutes.

Let that wave of positivity transport you to another dimension and seize the opportunity to do something completely different. Something new. Something special.

Meditate. Skip forward to chapter six. Call your girlfriend/boyfriend. Start learning Russian. Have a wank. Read friend Fukuoka's book *The One-Straw Revolution*. Water the garden.

Whatever you do, resist the temptation to check on your babies every few seconds. In fact it's probably best if you get out of the house altogether and go for a walk. As any harassed mother will tell you, fresh air will do you the world of good. You'll also find that the change of scene will stimulate your creative senses. It's amazing what emptying your head and doing something completely different, or just putting one foot in front of the other, will bring to mind.
To give you an idea of how useful taking a creative break can be in the production of a work of art, consider this: During the writing of this paragraph I went to the loo five times, made three cups of tea, ate two cookies and went for a walk. And just look at the result. Stunning, I'm sure you'll agree.

The one thing you shouldn't do whilst taking yourself out of the loop is use your phone or computer. Off is off. I should warn you now that John isn't much of a mobile telecommu-

IF YOU LOVE SOMETHING, SET IT FREE

nications kind of guy. GSOH, yes, GSM, hell no. The only thing he'd do with a Blackberry is bake it. His problem with technology nowadays is that we no longer have the patience to wait for something. We expect immediate answers to emails, text messages and further developments to come at us every second. And if we aren't instantly gratified, we get frustrated. And that doesn't do anyone any favours.

As we've come to appreciate, good things come to those who wait. In the good old days

I should warn you now that John isn't much of a technology person. The only thing he'd do with a Blackberry is bake it.

you'd think nothing of waiting a day or two for a response to a letter – sure, you'd look forward to the answer, and you'd run down to the mailbox every morning to see if it had come, but if not, you'd wait, safe in the knowledge that it would arrive in its own sweet time. And when that letter eventually arrived, you'd treasure it even more.

Don't worry about how quickly you're going to get somewhere; you'll get there in the end. Take the train instead of wasting your time in a traffic jam and seize the chance to read a book, or just look out of the window. Try talking to someone without checking your phone for messages every five seconds (even if your conversational partner appears to be particularly boring, dig deep and allow them a little longer to create a better impression). Don't refresh your browser window every minute to see if you've had any new emails - even if you're expecting a reply from that person you really, really, really want to hear from.

Maybe that's what Sting, deep in the depths of his personal meditation hut, was trying to say. The highest form of love is to set the object of your affections (and yourself) free. In other words: you need to walk away from the computer, or more pertinently, from the oven and chill the fuck out. At the end of the day, that's what your cookies will be doing, so just do like nature and go with the flow.

There
to

6 AFTERWARDS

are two sides
every cookie.

AFTERWARDS: THERE ARE TWO SIDES TO EVERY COOKIE

There are two sides to every cookie. Deep, huh?

We can think of no more graphic illustration of this principle than the one John himself gave us. We were just about to sit down to some tea and cookies at his place, when he dragged us back into the kitchen to clean his oven. To say that the enchantment he'd woven was shattered would be an understatement.

For, as you can imagine, if you bake a lot of cookies and are a living example for promoting the course of least action, you're not likely to have a particularly clean oven. But as we got to work, the lesson he was trying to teach us (eventually) sunk in. For everything good, there's something bad. It's impossible to talk about something good without a reference to something bad, since good and bad are joined together as parts of a mutual whole. For every cloud, there's a silver lining. For every grapefruit, there's a piece of butterscotch. And when the two combine, they give birth to something new. Grapefruit and butterscotch transform each other: like a wave in the ocean, every advance is followed by a retreat, and every rise transforms into a fall. Or, as John put it, to make something beautiful, you've got to do something ugly. In this particular instance, it's called cleaning up.

This principle is no more apparent at any other stage of the baking process than at this very moment. For if all's gone well, you're now the proud possessor of your heart's (or stomach's) desire: a tray full of delicious cookies. You could be forgiven for thinking that now is the time to enjoy the fruit of your labour and share them with your loved ones. Sadly, you'd be mistaken. That part still lies a little further ahead.

> To make something beautiful, you've got to do something ugly.

No one can live without having any impact on the environment, but if you offset anything you do that's bad (or dirty) with something you know is good, then John would certainly approve.

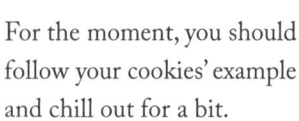

For the moment, you should follow your cookies' example and chill out for a bit.

Of course, you could skip ahead to the hedonistic blowout found at the end of our journey, as lots of people do. But, as you'll discover if you persevere with this chapter, learning to enjoy something means that sometimes you need to give a little back as well. Not because there's a universal bookkeeper, as other, lesser, "philosophers" might suggest. Contrary to popular belief, there's no one going round like a malevolent Santa Claus working out who's been a good and bad boy or girl. The reason it's good to give something back is because there's as much pleasure in giving as there is in receiving. What goes around, comes around. Giving is its own reward.

> He was certainly very happy once we'd cleaned his oven. Though we had the feeling that his desire to see his face in it was motivated more by his lack of a mirror than his concern with health and safety.

As no doubt you've come to expect from a man as enigmatic as John, there's another reason why he made… no, why he let us clean his oven. It was to illustrate in more depth the lesson learned in Chapter Four: By doing less, you achieve more. By getting us to clean his oven to teach us about karma, he was also reinforcing the "less is more" message, all the while doing nothing himself apart from kicking back and topping up his tan. We've said it before, and we'll say it again: What a guy.

A GOOD COOK IS A CLEAN COOK

John was also keen to impress on us the fact that "a good cook is a clean cook." And that means cleaning up after yourself: in the kitchen and beyond. It's a dirty job, but someone's got to do it. And unfortunately, as the creator of these heavenly treats, no matter how good they are and how much pleasure they give, it falls to you to clean up the mess you'll have inevitably made in the process. For just as it's impossible to make an omelette without breaking some eggs, it's almost as hard to make cookies without making a mess.

We realize that this might seem to clash slightly with the aforementioned lesson from Chapter Four, but no ideology is perfect. Not even John's. Sorry. Just see this particular contradiction as the logical extension of detachment. For once, and once only, we're going to ask you to be a little pragmatic and start scouring. This is as much for practical reasons as for ideological ones – if you don't clean your oven regularly, it's going to start affecting the flavour, and that's plain counter-productive. The secret is not to let cleaning get to you.

After all, there's a substantial reward lying in wait for you at the end of the (slightly grubby) rainbow. Even though we had to clean John's oven, he gave us a cookie at the end. Two actually. And lots of hugs. Plus the phone number of a particularly good Asian Massage Parlour (ask for *The Altman* if you drop by – a happy ending every time) in Modesto, California. And, as if we could forget, the recipe for his cookies.

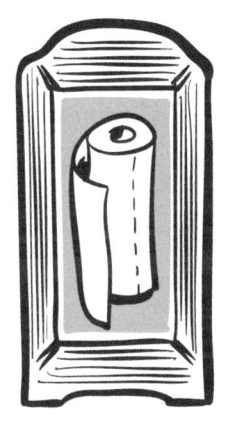

Basically, he said (at least this is what we think he said, it's difficult to be precise about what someone's saying when you've got your head in the oven): "What you're doing now is because of the decisions you've made and the things you've done in the past." Thus it follows that the future is made by what you do now. Which means that if you want to make a better tomorrow, you need to start taking care of it today.

Like, if you don't clean the oven now, then the next time you use it, it will just get worse. And if you leave it too long, then you'll be in real trouble. Especially if you're in the enviable position of running a restaurant or a public kitchen and Basil Fawlty's nightmare (no, not the Germans, the other one) comes to call.

Talking as one cook to another, we hope you've recognized that your responsibility isn't just confined to the kitchen. Although this is where most of your dominion lies, your influence also extends to the garden and the outside world: from the ingredients that go in your cookies to the power used in your kitchen. This doesn't mean that there's a karmic price to pay for enjoying nature's bounties – just that if you go a little way toward looking after them, you and everybody else will able to enjoy them for even longer.

Try and make yourself, your kitchen and your garden self-sufficient, and you'll be taking the first steps towards reducing your impact on the environment. Grow your own vegetables, recycle and precycle as much as you can and think twice about what you consume. Not in a puritanical, authoritarian, "live on bread and water alone" way, just in a "think about what you're doing" way.

No one can live without having any impact on the environment (even if you go to the remotest part of the Amazon forest to live with one of South America's few remaining uncontacted indigenous tribes, you'll have to fly to get there), but if you offset anything you do that's bad with something you know is good, then John would certainly approve (at least he was certainly very happy once we'd cleaned his oven, though we had the feeling that his desire to see his face in it was motivated more by his lack of a mirror than a concern for health and safety or the environment).

An easy way to pay Mother Nature back (with the added thrill that it's slightly legally dubious) is guerrilla gardening. It's a simple but wonderful idea. Take an abandoned or desolate space in a city and transform it into an urban paradise by planting flowers, trees and shrubs while people sleep. That's it. A couple of hours' gentle work, a few plants, a bit of love and a huge surprise that will give people pleasure for years to come. And best of all, once you've done your bit, you can let nature take care of the rest.

It's a simple but wonderful idea. Take an abandoned or desolate space in a city and transform it into an urban paradise by planting flowers, trees and shrubs while people sleep.

GUERILLA gardening

The good news is that cleaning up after yourself or your environment isn't really that hard. Of course, you could make it worse for yourself by trying to attach some extra, deeper meaning to the act and wondering what it all means and what you can really learn from it. To which the simple answer would be, use your imagination a little bit better. And get a life (and a different self-help book). But really and truly, even a task as mundane as washing up can be genuinely therapeutic if you create the right atmosphere.

YOU SET THE SCENE

Set the scene properly and every chore vaguely deserving of the name will become pleasure. Not in the tried, tested and rejected "see how many stamps you can lick in an hour, then try and beat your time" way, but in a "making life more bearable" kind of way. "Cleaning" has been traditionally seen as one of the most menial forms of labour, but not every tradition should be respected. John elevated it to the therapeutic and life-affirming rite it truly is. You know the score: Slip into your lucky silk pyjamas, put some music on, light some candles, sprinkle some rose petals around – and you might just find that it's possible to revel in the simple joy of taking something dirty and making it clean again. Although maybe that just shows that you need to get out more.

Most of the time we have to do something that we don't really want to do. So, rather than moan about it, why not grin and bear it? As my first boss told me numerous times, it takes less muscles to smile than to frown, so turn that frown upside down and put on a winning face! Then again, he once also informed me that there are no such things as problems, only solutions waiting to be found. And with a straight face, to boot. Make of that what you will. All I'll add is that at present there's still no *What would Anthony do?* to be found in a good bookshop near you. Or any bookstore, for that matter.

POLISHING OFF

For John, the most important thing is to be honest about what you do. There's no point protecting the rainforest in the Amazon if you're going to burn down lots of trees at home. Just like there's no point driving to the gym to go on a running

It's all good.

or a cycling machine when you could do everyone a favour and just go for a spin on a real bike instead. If you want to do something good, or something healthy, do it properly and wholeheartedly; otherwise you might as well not bother at all. Just be honest. And think about what you're doing.

After all this, if you still don't fancy doing any cleaning, then you could consider getting someone to do it for you. But you'd have to reward them suitably – possibly with something even more substantial than a cookie. Because if there's one thing we'd like you to take away from this chapter, it's that if you respect karma, karma will respect you. And if there's any doubt left in your mind, I'd like to refer you to another good ol' Dutch proverb: "Het komt voor de bakker." Which in English translates literally as: "It comes for the baker." Which to you and me means: "Everything's going to work out for the best." Or, as John might say, "It's all good."

And all because of the baker, man.

7 EATING

Bon

appétit!

EATING: BON APPÉTIT!

Now, where were we? Oh, yes… *You're now the proud possessor of your heart (or stomach's) desire: a tray of delicious cookies. You could be forgiven for thinking that it's now time to enjoy the fruit of your labour and share them with your loved ones.*

We hope you'll forgive us for that somewhat shameless attempt to whet your proverbial appetites, but it was important to take a step back. Just like the cookies, you needed to cool down for a while (at least 10 pages) before being ready to move on to the climax of our journey, where you and the cookie will become one.

THE FEAST
And you'll be pleased to hear that now it finally is time to do exactly that. To get your eat on. After all, that's what this book's about. The odyssey to create the perfect cookie might be an arduous and perilous path strewn with obstacles – not to mention a steep and unforgiving learning curve – but

there's always a light (and a mixed metaphor) at the end of the tunnel.

Because enjoying your hard-won homemade cookies is what we're all really here for. It's what we spent the vast majority of our time with John doing. Enjoying ourselves. Hanging out, shooting the breeze, chewing the cud (and some cookies). That's one thing we can certainly say John would do. Eat, drink and be merry. Okay, that's three, but who's counting?

It's our fervent wish that this is one part of the book that we can leave to your imagination. There's nothing worse than being told how to have fun by someone else. And although I'd like to think that we've come a long way together over the past six chapters, I wouldn't dare to tell you how you might best enjoy your cookies. Different strokes for different folks and all. So don't be fooled by the next heading. It's just something for the pedants (and editors) amongst us. Rest assured, we're going to let you eat your cookies in peace and relative quiet.

SERVING SUGGESTIONS

If you'd like to eat them all yourself, cool.

If you want to dunk them in milk, stick up them up your nose (or any other orifice), do your thing, but watch out for crumbs.

If you feel like giving them to someone else, nice.

The morning after, all we woke up with was a rather large hangover and the recipe for his cookies grasped tightly in our fingers.

If you decide to throw your friends (or pals, let's say pals) a tea party, or have a bake sale, even better.

They're your cookies to do with as you please. All we'd suggest is that you don't eat too many at the same time. And enjoy them as part of a balanced diet, obviously.

Because what's more important than eating the cookies themselves (yes, there is something that matters even more than that) is the galaxy of other delights that accompany the simple pleasure of consumption. The talking. The giving. The munching. The contented silences. The sighs. The "mmmms". The thank you's. The tea. The refills. The fireside. The little things that make it all worthwhile. So put the book down, and go and have some fun for John's sake.

There's enough time (and space) to worry about what John would do and how we can save the world later. I'd concentrate on saving your particular piece of the world one bite at a time. Starting with your dinner plate.

When you're sufficiently refreshed and your physical appetite has been sated, there'll be plenty of time to feed your spiritual side.

WHAT WOULD JOHN DO?
Ladies and gentlemen, it's time to finally answer the big question in life. The question you've been waiting at least a couple of hours for us to fully address. So without any further ado… Drum roll please…

Here, once and for all, is what John would do.

The good news is that it's more satisfying than a sled called *Rosebud* and a little bit more constructive than 42. And no, it's not 43. The even better news is that we're pleased to report that John did indeed give us the recipe for happiness. As you'd hope really, having invested so much of your precious time and money in this book.

The bad news is that after he had shared the meaning of life with us, we were so overcome with joy that we went straight out to celebrate with him, and the rest of the evening became a bit of a blur. Then the morning after, all we woke up with was a rather large hangover and the recipe for his cookies grasped tightly in our fingers. Initially, we were bitterly disappointed. But after much cogitation and even more soul searching, we came to the conclusion that the cookie recipe was as good an answer, if not better, than anything John

Even after all those Absinthe Bombs, I can remember it sounded pretty good.

could have presented us with the night before. What we held in our hands was indeed John's answer to life, the universe and everything.

MAKING COOKIES

The problem was that we'd placed such an extortionate value on the answer itself, that whatever it was that John had told us would only have been a disappointment. Although even after all those Absinthe Bombs, we can remember it sounded pretty good.

But the point is that the answer's irrelevant without knowing how you arrived there and what you learnt along the way. So if you really have skipped here from the beginning, then it's your loss. Sort of. For although you'll find the grand sum of John's accumulated wisdom here, you're missing all the details. Still, we're here now, and John would never throw anyone out of a party.

For a change, we're not trying to be pretentious or self-worthy here. All we're trying to say is that it's best to share the wealth. And your food. See, we figured out that the moral of the baking story is that you might have a lot on your plate in life, but there's always room for more. More friends, more cookies, more good times, more favours, more help, more smiles. Whatever you've got on your plate, share it.

John showed us that making cookies brings you closer to other people and to nature. It re-establishes your place in the world and strengthens it. How? By spreading the love. That's why John started baking cookies. That's why John passed on his baton to us. And that's what we're asking you to do now. Spread the love.

So the next time you're wondering what to do, think of John, yourself and others. Then everything should be a little clearer and the world a slightly better place. And if not, just relax. At the end of the day, it's not the be-all and end-all. Life is just what happens when the cookie crumbles. Some chunks will be bite-size, some will get trodden into the carpet, some you'll never see again (until you get round to cleaning behind the sofa). But if you just keep on baking, the chances of your seeing more of the cookie, and it tasting better, will increase.

All you can do is try and grab your piece while you can. Make it sweet. Sprinkle some special stuff on top. And see where it takes you.

Amen.

EPILOGUE

50

what now?

EPILOGUE

So what now?

That's exactly what we asked ourselves as we watched the sun set on Baker Beach after we'd said goodbye to John for the last time. Like us, you'll probably be feeling a bit empty at the moment, as you always do when someone leaves your life. Even if it's only until the next morning, or for a little while longer.

But you'll always have a little bit of John with you, whether it's in this book or beyond. And don't worry about him. He'll be fine. All he'd want you to do is take the wisdom you find strewn amongst these pages and sow the seeds of love wherever you go.

We'll eat to that.

WHAT WOULD JOHN DO?

WHAT WOULD JOHN DO?

This is a copy of the recipe that John gave us for his cookies. The original is preserved by the Smithsonian Institution in the National Museum of American History, Washington D.C.

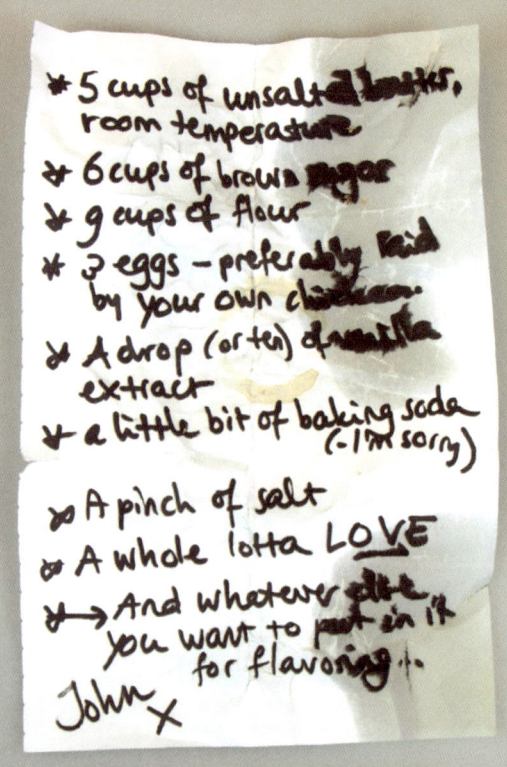

For those unable to decipher the lethal combination of John's scrawl and our greasy fingerprints, we've included the recipe in a slightly more legible form below.

5 cups of unsalted butter, room temperature
6 cups of brown sugar
9 cups of flour
3 eggs (preferably laid by your own chicken)
A drop (or ten) of vanilla extract
A little bit of baking soda (I'm sorry)

A pinch of salt
A whole lotta love.
And whatever else you want to put in for flavoring…

John x

THIS IS HOW WE DO IT

Put the butter in a big bowl. Beat it until it's smooth and creamy. Whack the sugar in until it goes nice and fluffy. Then add the eggs in one at a time, keeping the beat as steady as Ringo. When that's all in, add the vanilla, and yep, beat it.

After that, you can treat yourself to a cup of tea, before mixing the flour, baking soda and salt together in a separate bowl. Once that's done, add that to the egg mixture, beat it, before introducing the stars of your show into the mix (whatever they may be) and beating it all together until you're bored or the batter's perfectly consistent, whichever comes first.

You'll be pleased to hear that marks the end of the beating. Celebrate this by preheating the oven to 375° Fahrenheit and getting a baking tray out of the cupboard.
Dollop your batter gently on to the tray, before placing your babies reverently in the oven.

Take them out when they're golden brown around the edges, then leave them to cool on a wire rack (preferably not in the oven).

Stick the kettle on. Call your friends. Enjoy!

ACKNOWLEDGEMENTS

Love goes out to: Jeroen Klaver, aka Shamrock, for the illustrations and entertaining company. Hajo de Boer and Onno Lixenberg, for finding John in the first place. Karl Chillmaid, for his patience and diligence in editing the text and being a generally all round nice guy. Tom Georgi, for going through the text with his customary (and endearing) frankness. Tommaso Minnetti, for nothing.
Nobody Beats The Drum, for inspiring me to quit my job and get back to bed. Everyone at Gummo, for being the best people to work with in the whole world ever. Paul Turken, the original Yogi Bear. Rudolf and Bionda from BIS, for all their help and enthusiasm in giving this book to the world. Emiel Steenhuizen, Larry Burns and Mighty Mike, for bringing John to our screens so beautifully. Nard, for spreading the love through the internet.
Frank Lubbers; Jaques and Els van Strien, for making John Altman Cookies taste so damn good. And everybody else whose accumulated wisdom has been channelled to produce this book.

Love Will x